Instant Google Map Maker Starter

Learn what you can do with Google Map Maker and get started with building your first map

Limoke Oscar

[PACKT]

PUBLISHING

BIRMINGHAM - MUMBAI

Instant Google Map Maker Starter

First published: March 2013

Production Reference: 1120313

Published by Packt Publishing Ltd.
Livery Place
35 Livery Street
Birmingham B3 2PB, UK.

ISBN 978-1-84969-528-2

www.packtpub.com

Credits

Author

Limoke Oscar

Reviewer

Jabran Rafique

Acquisition Editor

Usha Iyer

Commissioning Editor

Priyanka Shah

Technical Editor

Dominic Pereira

Project Coordinator

Sherin Padayatty

Proofreader

Mario Cecere

Production Coordinator

Prachali Bhiwandkar

Cover Work

Prachali Bhiwandkar

Cover Images

Conidon Miranda

About the Author

Limoke Oscar has been a member of the Google Map Maker community since 2009. He completed his undergraduate studies in 2012 with a Bachelor of Science in Geomatic Engineering and Geospatial Information Systems from the Jommo Kenyatta University of Agriculture and Technology in Nairobi, Kenya. He hopes to pursue a postgraduate degree in the same field in the near future. He has worked as a Google Apps Technical Support Associate at Google Kenya and is currently a Geospatial Information Systems (GIS) Consultant running a geo solutions firm that he cofounded—Geoglobal East Africa Ltd. He is an avid user and contributor to Google Map Maker and other Google Geo tools and has made extensive contributions to Google Map Maker. In 2011, he was awarded a Distinguished Map Maker certificate by Google. He believes in giving back to his community through knowledge and technology as tools of empowerment. He does so by volunteering for the Wikimedia Foundation and the One Laptop Per Child (OLPC) Foundation.

I am indebted to Beryl Samba, for her moral support and for the free English grammar tips and consultation all through the process of writing this book. Without her encouragement, support, and lessons, this piece would never have seen the printer beyond page one. Thank you so much.

I would like to thank Priyanka as well, for scouting and being able to sniff my work from way across the world through my blog and for the endless support and kind introductions to all the wonderful folks at Packt Publishing.

About the Reviewer

Jabran Rafique is an experienced web developer, designer, and a volunteer to Google Map Maker. He also serves as an Advocate of this product since 2011. He has recently completed his post graduation in Computer Science with focus on Web Development from Staffordshire University in England. He normally works on building his own applications, which are helpful and useful for everyday use. He is looking forward to eventually becoming an entrepreneur. He also has plans to do a doctorate at some point. Being part of the Google Map Maker Advocate program and relevant works, he has organized, spoken, and attended many conferences internationally as well as supervised training sessions on locations and online to guide and encourage mapping volunteers to produce helpful digital maps using this platform, especially for developing countries.

I would like to thank Packt Publishing for considering me as a reviewer for this helpful guide for interested new mappers. I would also like to thank all those active volunteers at Google Map Maker forums, social media groups, and their private discussion boards from where I could gain all the experience through which I could review this book, make it more helpful and explainable for readers, and as well as my family and close friends for being understandable and supportive—whom I ditched for a short while to concentrate on this work.

www.packtpub.com

Support files, eBooks, discount offers and more

You might want to visit www.PacktPub.com for support files and downloads related to your book.

Did you know that Packt offers eBook versions of every book published, with PDF and ePub files available? You can upgrade to the eBook version at www.PacktPub.com and as a print book customer, you are entitled to a discount on the eBook copy. Get in touch with us at service@packtpub.com for more details.

At www.PacktPub.com, you can also read a collection of free technical articles, sign up for a range of free newsletters and receive exclusive discounts and offers on Packt books and eBooks.

packtLib.packtpub.com

Do you need instant solutions to your IT questions? PacktLib is Packt's online digital book library. Here, you can access, read and search across Packt's entire library of books.

Why Subscribe?

- ✦ Fully searchable across every book published by Packt
- ✦ Copy and paste, print and bookmark content
- ✦ On demand and accessible via web browser

Free Access for Packt account holders

If you have an account with Packt at www.PacktPub.com, you can use this to access PacktLib today and view nine entirely free books. Simply use your login credentials for immediate access.

Table of Contents

Instant Google Map Maker Starter

Welcome to the *Instant Google Map Maker Starter*. This book has been especially created to provide you with all the information that you need to get set up with Google Map Maker. You will learn the basics of Google Map Maker, get started with creating your own Maps, and discover some tips and tricks for using Google Map Maker.

This document contains the following sections:

So, what is Google Map Maker? – find out what Google Map Maker actually is, what you can do with it, and why it's so great.

System Requirements – learn how and what you need to get started with Google Map Maker with the minimum fuss and then get up and running in no time.

Quick Start – this section will show you how to perform one of the core tasks of Google Map Maker—mapping the places you love and know. Follow the steps to create your own map features, which will be the basis for most of your work in Google Map Maker.

Top features you need to know about – here you will learn how to perform five key tasks with the most important features of Google Map Maker. By the end of this section you will be able to add features, edit features, review edits, browse features, manage neighborhoods, and share edits.

People and places you should get to know – every community project is centered on a community. This section provides you with many useful links to the project page and forums, as well as a number of helpful articles, tutorials, blogs, discussion groups, and social media forums (Twitter, Google plus, Facebook) for Google Map Maker super-contributors.

So, what is Google Map Maker?

Google Map Maker is a collaborative and community-driven mapping environment or a tool that allows individuals to add or edit their local geographical information including local businesses, roads and footpaths, schools, entertainment spots, parking lots, hotels, campuses, and much more. This geographical information can then be pushed to Google Maps and other products such as Google Earth and Google Maps Mobile. Additional information such as business name addresses, phone numbers, road names, conditions, access, and grade levels can also be added to improve the quality of the local map and for listing in Google Locals—a Geo listing directory for local businesses by Google. With Google Map Maker, you can:

✦ Add places of interest such as your hotels, cinemas, schools, and more

✦ Edit and update details for existing places

✦ Get driving directions and also help in making them more accurate

✦ See what your peers are mapping in specific areas

By sharing information about the places you know and love in your town or area, you ensure that the map accurately reflects the world around you. This is true, as local users know their local areas better than anyone else. Any edits/updates made in Google Map Maker are subject to review by other people with knowledge of the area. With time, as an individual makes more correct edits and updates to Map Maker, he becomes a trusted reviewer and editor and thus some of his/her edits will be published automatically without any need for review. This, however, doesn't mean that other mappers cannot revert or review his edits should they feel they are incorrect; the edits can be reviewed as incorrect and thus unpublished or corrected by other mappers.

With Google Map Maker, you can map an entire neighborhood, town, campus, or even an entire country for the whole world to see, as shown in the next screenshot:

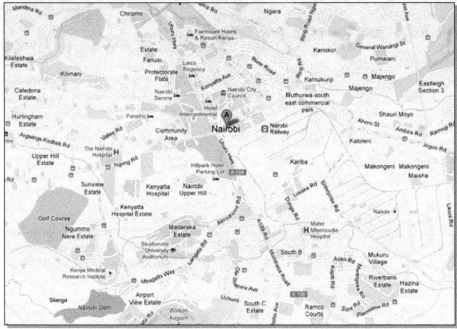

A well-mapped town in Kenya

You can make edits using Google Map Maker in over 200 countries and regions around the world. See an example of a township in Kenya mapped by avid mappers (preceding screenshot) and Sri Lanka before and after using Google Map Maker (following screenshot).

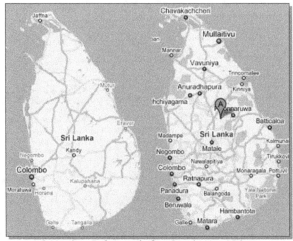

Sri Lanka—Before and after Google Map Maker

System requirements

Assuming local expertise, knowledge, and interest in your area, it is fairly easy to get started with Map Maker. You need a computer, a good Internet connection, and a modern browser to start mapping with Google Map Maker. Recommended modern browsers that provide best experience include:

- **Microsoft Internet Explorer (IE) 9.0 and later (for Windows)**: Can be downloaded from `http://www.microsoft.com/windows/ie/downloads/default.mspx`

- **Firefox 3.6 and later (for Windows, Mac, and Linux)**: Can be downloaded from `http://www.mozilla.org/products/firefox/`

- **Safari 3.1 and later (for Mac and Windows)**: Can be downloaded from `http://www.apple.com/safari`

- **Google Chrome (for Windows and Mac)**: Can be downloaded from `http://www.google.com/chrome`

You can make use of secondary data and information such as topographical maps, town plans, GPS data, and so on, but remember all the input has to be done manually and that the data should not violate any copyright or personal privacy. Note that Google Map Maker enforces a strict policy where addition of personal and private data is prohibited and, in most cases, is removed/reported instantly by Regional Expert Reviewers or Advocates.

Lastly, remember that Google Map Maker is available in 185 countries. You can create/edit features in Google Map Maker from only these countries. For a full list of supported countries, visit `www.support.google.com/mapmaker/answer/1555415?hl=en`.

Quick start

Quick start—this section will show you how to perform one of the core tasks of Google Map Maker—mapping the places you love and know. Follow the steps to create your own map features, which will be the basis of most of your work in Google Map Maker.

Common issues in Google Map Maker

Before we get started, it's worth taking into consideration some of the known issues with Google Map Maker:

✦ Map Maker interface does not usually come fully translated into all languages at the same time. UI translations are usually rolled out gradually and are a part of another community-driven effort. This project is accessible at `http://www.google.com/transconsole/giyl/chooseProject`. Note that some of the languages—for example, Urdu despite being translated completely—still are not available in Map Maker UI.

✦ Map Maker has not been verified for compatibility with Internet Explorer 7 and earlier versions of IE.

Google Map Maker is accessed by firing the URL `http://www.google.com/mapmaker`. To access and get started with Map Maker, you must have a Google Account in order to start making and submitting edits. A **Google Account** is a unified sign-in system that provides access to a variety of free Google consumer products such as Gmail, Google Groups, Google Maps, Google Wallet, AdWords, AdSense, and so on. Think of a Google Account as a single Google sign-in, made up of an e-mail address (any e-mail address, does not have to be a Gmail) and a password of your choice, that gives you access to all the Google products under your own profile.

Create your Google Account by visiting `https://accounts.google.com/SignUp` if you would like to use another e-mail address. If you already have a Gmail account, please sign in from the left pane when you visit `http://www.google.com/mapmaker`, as shown here:

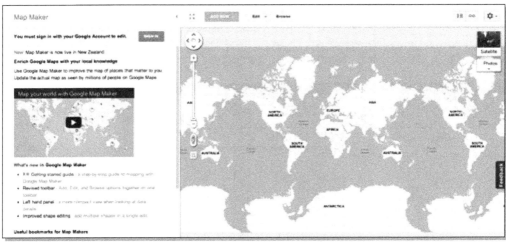

The Map Maker interface during the first visit

The Map Maker interface

The Google Map Maker interface is simple, intuitive, and easy to use. It has standard graphical icons that help you navigate around the tools and functionalities. Let us take a closer look at it:

A first-time login to Map Maker starts by displaying a tutorial to quickly take you through the key features of Google Map Maker. You can navigate your way through the quick tutorial by going back and forth using the respective forward and back arrows. You can close the quick tutorial and get started with making edits right away by clicking on the **X** icon on top. Don't worry, you can always access the tutorial later, as will be explained later in this book.

The Map Maker UI

Let us take a detailed look at the Map Maker interface, I have tried to subdivide it based on the main functionalities and purposes of the tools. Key tools/sections that you need to know are highlighted and clearly labeled as well. I have named them based strictly on the functionality and this is by no means the conventional way of doing so.

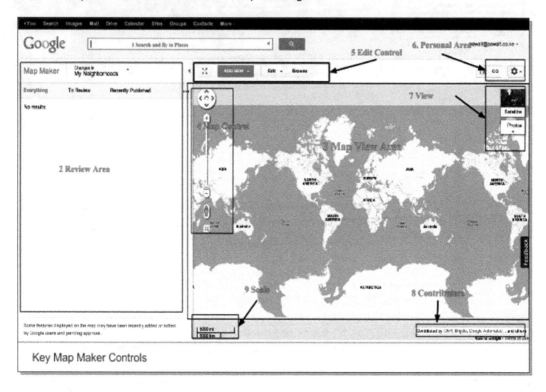

Key Map Maker Controls

Let us take a quick deep dive into the tools and see what each section serves:

Search

The search area allows you to search and fly to places you want to in Map Maker in an instant. It works just like Google Search, only that it returns a map zoomed to the area/business you queried. Try it. Type the name of your city and hit *Enter*. This comes in handy when, on visiting Google Map Maker, the default load is not defaulting to your current location much as it should or just when you want to make edits and/or reviews in some other area you are familiar with or just to view and visit places. Take a look at the following search query:

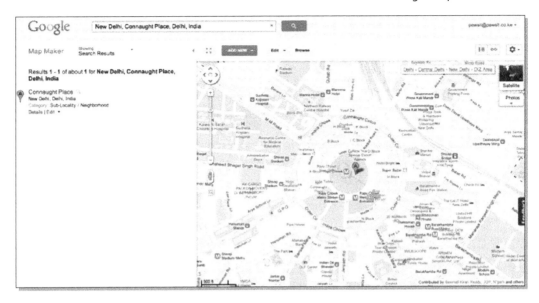

Review area

This is the area that displays your own recent edits as well as displaying edits happening within your neighborhood that you created or are based on your location. You can switch between the tabs based on the functionality that you want; the different tabs are explained as follows:

✦ **Everything**: This tab is like a channel stream or timeline. Shows the recent activities in terms of new edits, reviews, or comments by you and other mappers within the neighborhood view of the map, that is, the current location of the map that is in view. See the following example:

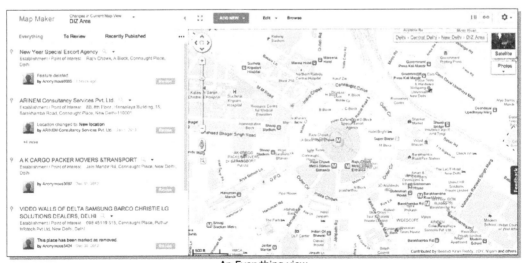

An Everything view

✦ **To Review**: This area only highlights the edits whose reviews are pending.

✦ **Recently Published**: Streams all those recent edits, which have been approved and published. You can, however, still contest these edits or correct them if they are incorrect.

✦ **Filter by Category**: Just next to the **Recently Published** tab, you will find a three-dot tab that allows you to expand this section. This section is the filter section and gives you the power to filter by categories the actions, places, and edits you would like to perform. For instance, you may just be interested in (re)viewing road and line features or the chronological order of the edits being made in the locale.

Filter by Category

Map view area

This is the area where the Google Maps loads in order to allow you to perform the operations and edits that you want. The map view usually defaults to your current location when you visit http://www.google.com/mapmaker.

Map controls

These tools allow you to control the view of the map. They allow you to pan, zoom, and view **Street View** for supported cities. Let's take a look at what and how each of the tools comes in handy:

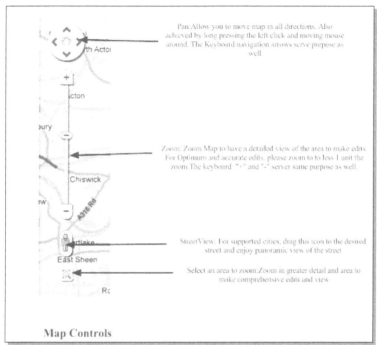

Map controls

Edit control

This is the area that allows you to make new edits to Map Maker and correct existing ones as well. You can create new point, line, and polygon features by exploring the **Add New** tab. Note that the tools will change according to the main tool selected. You can also edit existing point, line, polygon, and direction features by exploring the **Edit** tab. We will take a deep dive into this section a little later in this book.

Personal/User area

I call this the personal area, because it allows you to personalize your Map Maker through custom settings and adding labs (experimental features that are still under testing and development). Labs allow you to extend the normal functionality of Map maker. This section also allows you to share your edits, directions, and maps with your friends by generating a unique URL for it. Create and make changes to your Map Maker profile, access **Help** and discussion forums, report a bug, and as well as submit feedback to the Google Maker team by using these tools.

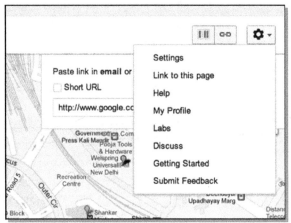

Personal user area

View

The **View** section allows you to switch between the different layers of Google Map Maker—**Satellite** and **Map**. In a **Map** view, you only get to view the map details created by users, whereas in Satellite view, you can see the map elements overlaying the satellite imagery provided to Google by various satellite imagery providers and partners. This is the best layer to use when making edits as it allows you to draw/trace over the edits from the satellite imagery to creating the features in a process called **digitization** in Cartography terms. It is actually the backbone of this community-driven project. Users have to align everything from satellite imagery to points feature, line features, and polygon features for better accuracy; otherwise their edits may be denied or delayed in the reviewing process. You can add more layers such as photos, which will display edits/features alongside the photos uploaded among other features. To switch between and add layers, simply click on it and the **Map** view will be populated with the layer(s) of your selection.

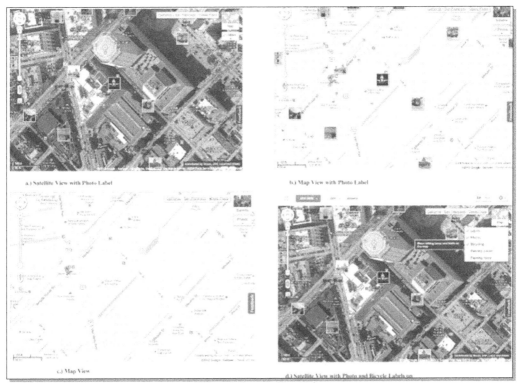

Different views in Map Maker

Contributors

The Contributors' segment displays all the contributors who have made a substantial number of edits on the area of the **Map** view. It displays the contributors' preferred nicknames (set during the signing-up stage). If you click on any nickname, it takes you to their respective Map Maker profiles showing their edits and badges earned.

Scale

This section will show us the display scale of the map as we zoom in and out.

Top features you need to know about

Now let us get down to the real use of Google Map Maker. In this section, we will explore the core tools and functionalities of Google Map Maker that will help us to move from being a newbie to a professional mapper and reviewer in Google Map Maker. Remember all your edits and reviews, however minor, are always credited to your profile.

I am sure, by now, you must have gained some insight into how Google Map Maker works—Google Map Maker has a community of voluntary mappers who have a desire to map the places they know and love. However, since recently Google has been integrating its location services in search and across their product line, businesses have seen the need for them to increase their online visibility through listings in Google Geo tools such as Google Places, Google Maps, Google Maps Mobile, and so on. In a bid to make the best use of these services, businesses are also putting up their business in Google Maps through Google Map Maker. This is perhaps the easiest and quickest way to add a business listing to Google Geo products as we will see in a short while.

Similarly, Google Maps created by local mappers are increasingly finding use in humanitarian crises. A case in point is the response to the Mapping appeal by Pakistani Map Maker volunteers Omer Sheikh and Jabran Rafique to a series of landslides that occurred after floods that hit Atta Abad, a semi-autonomous region of Pakistan, causing loss of lives and blocking the Hunza River in January 2010. Omer Sheikh and Jabran Rafique come out strongly mapping the area and putting an appeal to the entire world to help improve the rescue effort through accurate mapping of the region. As Omer put it in the Google Lat Long Blog (`http://google-latlong.blogspot.com/2010/06/map-makers-respond-to-pakistan.html`):

> *From the onset of the disaster, the international community seemed to be hardly aware of the situation. Worst...I was unable to locate on a map where Atta Abad was! As a mapper, my first appeal went out to the Google Map Maker team, and Google Maps Pakistan.*

They went ahead and built a website (`http://www.local.com.pk/hunza/`) making use of the Google Maps API to visualize the data and together with the Google Map Maker Team and the UN, made the data available for download publically, which helped with the humanitarian crisis. A similar appeal was made for the Horn of Africa Conflict in 2011, see `http://goo.gl/G71Yv`.

Please note that the best way you can get a business or an incorrectly-placed feature in Google Maps (or correct the same) is by editing or reviewing it in Google Map Maker. In adding and editing features in Google Map Maker, it's worth mentioning that geographic features in a map can be represented in two different data formats:

✦ **Raster data**: The representation of geographic information as regular grid cell(s). Think of this as the background satellite image upon which we will be creating maps and features.

✦ **Vector data**: The representation of geographic objects with the basic elements of points, lines, and polygons. Think of this as the point, linear, and polygonal features; we will very shortly learn how to create these features in Google Map Maker. Point and polygons can be used to represent the same features, but at a different scale and depending on the level of detail desired.

We will be adding vector data (hotels, roads, paths, cafes, shopping malls) to the already provided raster data (satellite image) by Google. The core features and operations we are going to learn how to quickly perform are:

Adding new Features to Google Maps

As just discussed previously, the features to be added to Google Maps are either going to be in a point, linear, or a polygon form. Let's go through the process of adding each of these features to Google map maker:

Points or Points of Interest (POI)

POI could be a business, a cafe, a hotel, or even an apartment. Follow these steps to add POI to Google Map Maker:

1. To add a POI on Google Map Maker, fire `http://www.google.com/mapmaker`.

    By default, it should load the current location you are accessing the Internet from. If that's where you would like to Map, proceed. If not, search the place you want to map in the search bar as earlier discussed.

2. Zoom in on the map to level **19** (the **Zoom** bar has 20 units), so that you can map the POI to a high detail. Add the satellite layer by clicking on **Satellite** in the upper-left corner within the **Map** view area, so that you can trace the feature you want at pinpoint accuracy, as shown in the following screenshot:

3. Then click on the **Add a Place** drop-down, select the category—your POI falls under—from the given Category:

4. If the POI does not fall under any of the given categories, click on **Type to select from over 2000+ categories** and enter the feature's category and name:

5. Continue to toggle up the info panel on the left, this allows you to enter more descriptive information about the POI such as the telephone, website, working hours, and so on and then click on **Save**:

Congratulations, you have added a new POI onto Google Maps. The feature will be reviewed by other Google Map makers and upon confirmation, will be reviewed and published in Google Maps. You can continue to add more POI as you await review of your edits. Remember about the private policy regarding personal and private information. Do not add features such as houses, private mobile numbers, private e-mail addresses, and so on. Such edits may be denied or delayed in the reviewing process.

Polygons

Businesses and other POIs can be added as polygons based on the level of generalization needed. For instance, tracing our building, property, and forest boundaries is a simple way of adding POIs by polygon.

To add a polygonal feature in Google Map Maker, follow these steps:

1. From the home screen of the Map Maker UI, click on **Add New**.

2. Select **Add Building Outlines,** as shown in the following screenshot:

3. Select the category in which the feature falls under and proceed to trace out the feature within the map view; trace till you get back to the initial point.

4. Notice the pop-up box that pops up on the bottom-left corner of the screen when you start drawing the polygon. It provides simple tips and instructions on how best to draw your feature. Also note the **Draw** menu at the upper-right corner that toggles up. It provides additional tools for editing and changing the polygon feature.

5. To close the polygon, double-click on the last/starting point upon which a detail pane is toggled up for you to add descriptive information on the feature, as shown here:

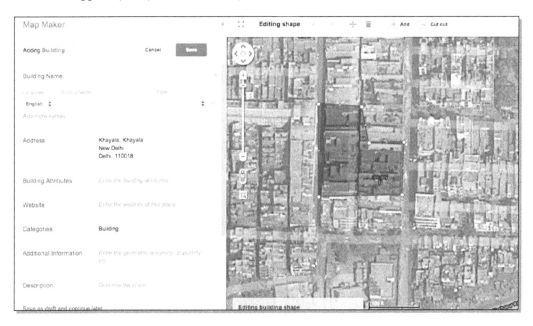

6. While still adding the descriptive details, notice the new menu toggled at the top of the map view area. This menu allows you to edit the polygon that you have traced. You can move the feature to some other location; you can cut a hole through it in order to create an **Island feature** within this feature. An example of a cut made within a larger polygon feature is shown here:

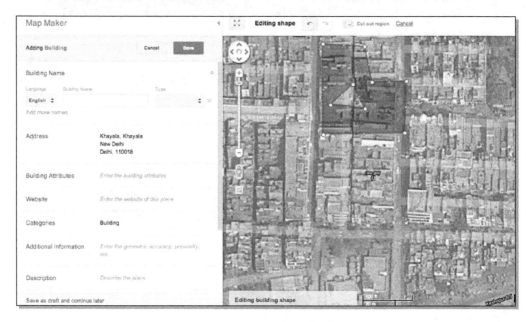

7. Add the details, description, and address that define the polygonal feature as well. click **Save**. Continue to add more features as you await approval/moderation of your feature.

Lines

Linear features such as roads, railway lines, or trails/path are perhaps the easiest to add to Google Map Maker. Primarily, because you do not need to provide all the details for your edit to go through. Simply tracing and creating a road or a trail is good enough even if you do not have other key details such as name, type of road, and so on. To add a line feature, follow these steps:

1. On the home screen of Map Maker, click on **Add New**.

2. Select **Add Roads, Rivers, Railways** from the drop-down, as shown here:

3. Proceed to add the category within which your feature falls and off you go to create it.

4. Click on the starting point of your feature and carefully proceed to trace/digitize the feature outline, paying closer attention to the curves and turning points:

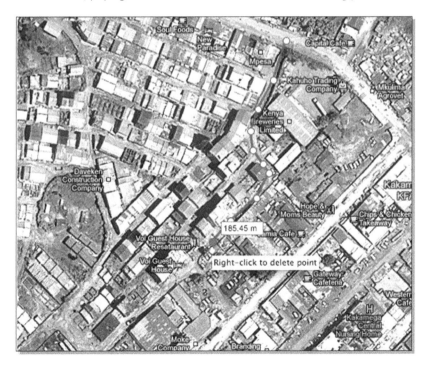

5. Should you make a wrong point, don't worry, you can always undo with *Ctrl* + *Z* on Windows, *Cmd* + *Z* on Mac, or you can as well right-click on the point and select **Delete this point** and proceed making your correct trace points, as shown in the following screenshot:

6. Double-click on the end point to finish your feature and add the relevant details, if available and appropriate, such as road name, road attributes such as number of lanes, dividers, surface type, or access then hit **Save**, as shown here:

7. Although adding the descriptive information about line features is not compulsory, it is important to note that these are the features that make the directions work accordingly. Details such as road priority, number of lanes, average speed, surface types, and road conditions are some of the variables that the directions and navigation (wherever supported) take into consideration before optimizing the best route.

8. Some type of line features, for example, river, water bodies require mixing two types of drawing features—line feature and polygon feature. This would involve drawing the line part as a line feature and then when it's a lake, for instance, you draw the polygon as two separate features but with the same name.

Directions

Directions are not much of a feature in Google Maps. Based on the existing features created in Google Map Maker, you can create/determine the directions between any of them. To create a direction in Google Map Maker, it's important to know that you need at least two existing features in Google Map Maker.

1. To get started, find/identify the two points that you need to create directions between.

2. Right-click on one of the features and select how you want the directions—either to the feature or from the feature—as shown in the following screenshot:

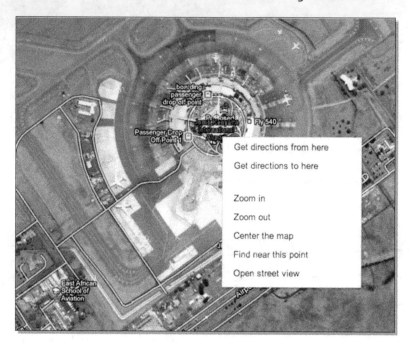

3. Type in the name of the destination/current location, depending on how you want your directions and select what kind of directions you want: **By Car (Driving), Walking**, or **Bicycle (Cycling)** by selecting from the respective icons and then create the directions. A route map is created with clear turn-by-turn instructions between the selected destinations, as shown here:

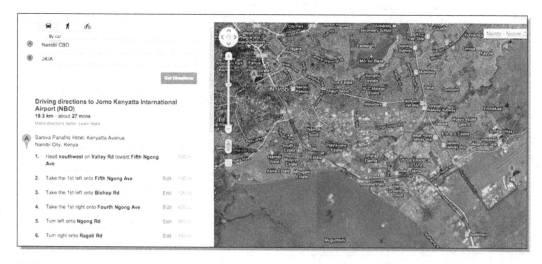

Editing existing features

Editing features in Google Map Maker involves two things:

+ Editing feature location for a wrongfully-placed feature
+ Editing feature-descriptive data for inaccuracy

Either way, the procedure for doing so is similar and the same as the procedure for adding new features. It involves identifying/spotting the inaccuracies or incorrectness in a feature and then proceeding to Google Map Maker, to search, identify the feature, and correct the inaccuracy. Let us take a look at how to edit each class of feature as discussed previously:

Points/ POI

Assuming you have spotted an erroneously-mapped feature while you were either adding new features or while using one of other Google Geo Platforms, the way to go about to correct it is simple; here it is:

1. Visit the Google Map Maker application by visiting `http://www.google.com/mapmaker`.

2. Find the feature through the search area as previously shown. The feature(s) related to your query will be populated in the map view area; identity the one you want to edit.

3. Click on it within the map view area and select **Edit**, as shown here:

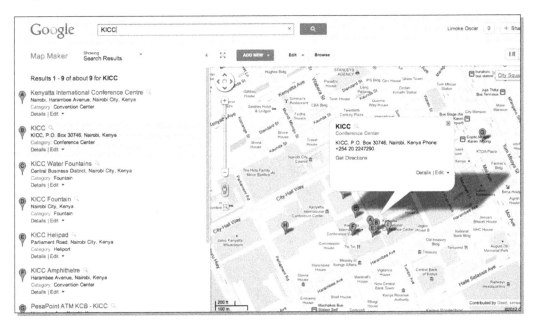

4. Select what/how you want to edit the feature:

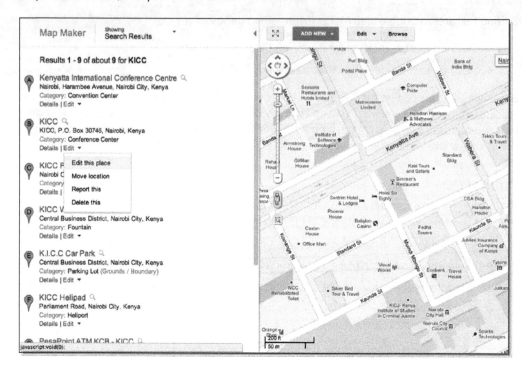

- **Edit this place**: This option will allow you to edit the feature details and descriptive information as shown here:

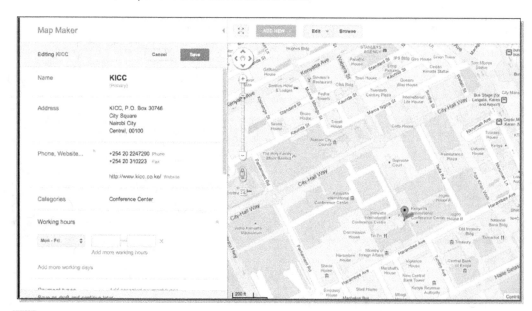

- ○ **Move location**: If the feature is incorrectly placed in its location, you can drag and move it to its correct location by using this option:

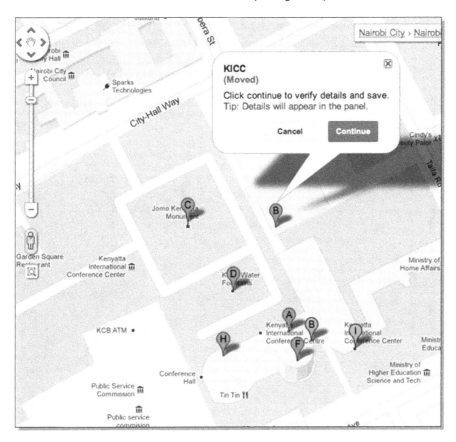

° **Report this**: Use this option if you would just like to report a feature as wrongfully placed or with incorrect details to draw the attention of the community to correct it appropriately. Provide the reason as to why you are reporting this feature by selecting one of the reasons: **Spam Edit, Violating Privacy, Trademarks, Duplicity,** and so on. You can only provide a single reason and you must provide a short description remark for the reason of reporting, as shown in the following screenshot:

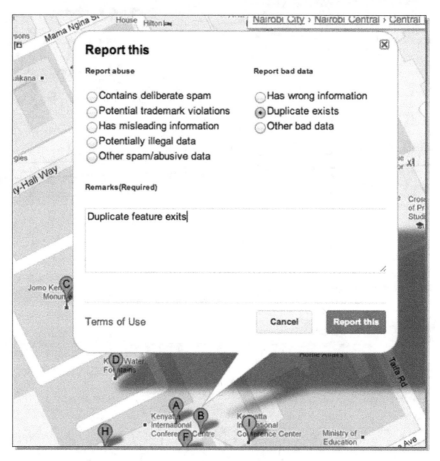

° **Delete this** : Delete a feature if you are sure it is either incorrectly placed, is a duplicate feature, or for any of the reasons listed here:

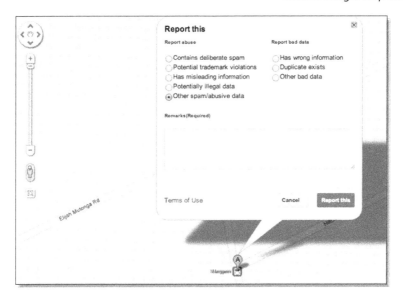

Lines

Editing linear features such as roads or rivers involves either fixing the missing links, correcting wrong turns within the feature, or altogether deleting a wrongfully-drawn feature. Note that to edit a feature, you must search for it by name and then when it is populated in the map view area, you can edit it. Once highlighted, on the left pane, select **Edit** and select what or the way by which you want to edit the feature:

+ **Edit this route**: This option takes you to the route after which you can correct what is incorrect.

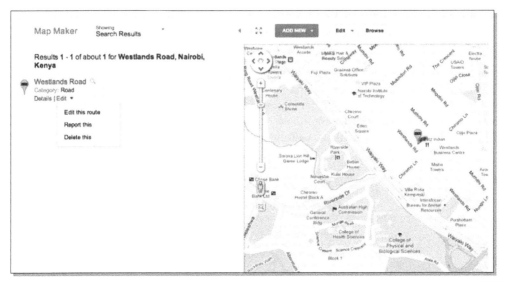

◆ Either the details or the route itself could be incorrect. We can correct this by hard-pressing the mouse/touchpad along the incorrect points and dragging each point to the correct place as shown in the following screenshot:

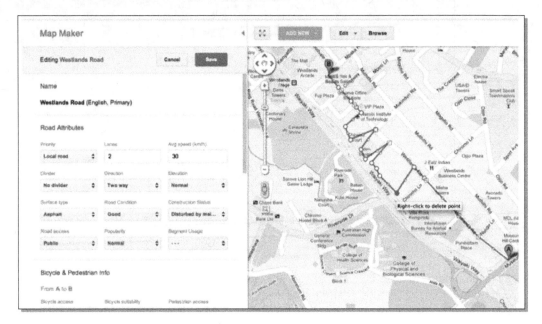

◆ **Report this** and **Delete this** work as earlier discussed. You can report a route as incorrect and provide the reasons as well as delete it for the same reason.

Polygons

Basically, polygonal features are similar to point features but at a different generalization or scale. So editing them is very similar to the points, assuming you have identified the error either in the boundaries of the feature or the details.

Reviewing edits in Google Map Maker simply involves checking on the edits made by other mappers and agreeing/disagreeing with the feature's location and/or the descriptive information provided. This is the simple concept that insures reflection of the features on the ground and as seen by the locals within the neighborhood. Anyone can dispute on the appearance or accuracy of features if it aggrieves them and/or infringes on their personal privacy.

Reviewing and moderating edits/features

Reviewing edits is very easy and just like edits, reviews also are credited to your profile contributions in Google Map Maker. There are three ways by which you can get started in making reviews. The upper-left pane of the Google Map Maker displays the various activities happening in Google Map Maker, including edit count, reviews, and so on. The activity view stream is as shown here:

We can start our reviewing through these activity streams, as explained here:

✦ **Everything**: This stream shows all the activities within the current map view of the Map Maker Scrolling through his section allows you to see all the activities including the new features created, edit's pending review, and the reasons. You can review directly from here, but it's best to move to the next tab, which is explained in the next point.

✦ **To Review**: This is the section that allows you to view all those edits made within the current map view that need review. Here is how you do this:

    1. Simply scroll and identify the features you would like to review.

    2. Click **Review**. This opens up the feature within the map view:

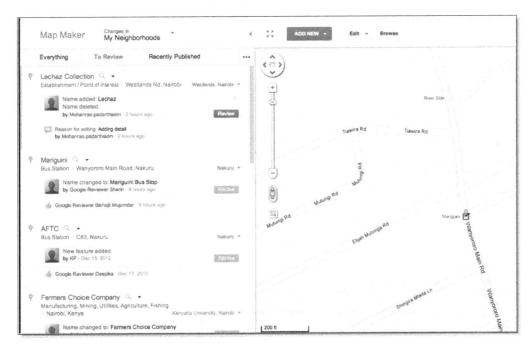

3. Go through the feature location and the details carefully and when convinced that it's correct, go ahead, agree, and review, that is, agree that changes are correct:

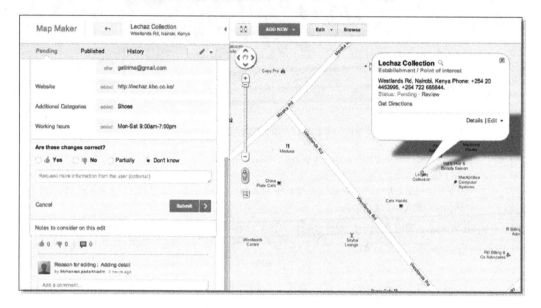

4. If not, provide the reason for rejecting the edit and/or request for more information from the user through the remarks section and submit as shown here:

✦ **Browse by Filters**: This is the hidden function that is accessed if you expand the left
  pane by clicking on the three dots, as shown here:

This section allows you to view the types of edits through a simple filter. Say, you just
want to review point features and arrange them from oldest to newest or want to do
line features only, then this is the tool for you. Try it out.

Browse features

You can browse or explore places in Google Map Maker fairly easily. This is just like you would
do in other Google Geo platforms such as Google Maps and Google Earth. After all, most of
the features/places found in all the other Google Geo platforms for most of the world are
contributed by volunteers through Google Map Maker. Browsing features/places in all simplicity
involves searching for the features in the **Search** pane and tour query will be displayed in the
map view area. However, **Browse** feature is much more than just a simple search tool. The
advanced feature of **Browse** enables users to find detailed and custom maps. Some of such
examples are showcased at `http://geography.pk/_en/2011/05/08/an-overview-of-`
`mapped-pakistan-at-google-map-maker/`. Sometimes, the same feature may exist multiple
times or under different/alternative names.

Sharing edits on Google Plus

Would you like to share your edits or any features from Google Map Maker with your friends? Don't worry, it's very easy. You can share your edits as you edit or review them or even share other people's edits. Simply search for the feature that has been published, or the one you have just edited, or is in the map view area and click on the **Share** icon at the upper-right corner of the map view. The highlighted feature will be posted to your Google Plus account, if you have one, to all your friends and the public if you want to:

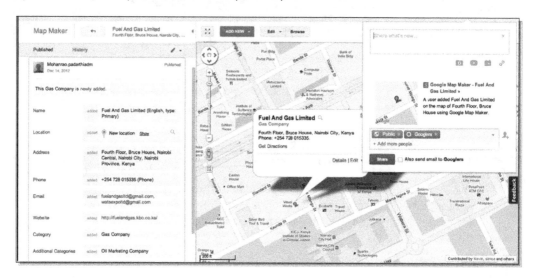

People and places you should get to know

Every open source project is centered on a community. This section provides you with many useful links to the project's page and forums, as well as a number of helpful articles, tutorials, blogs, discussion groups, and social media forums (Twitter, Google Plus, Facebook) for Google Map Maker contributors. You can, however, navigate your way to the majority of all these forums and resources form the central **Map Your World Community** from here: `http://goo.gl/imKJ2`.

Google Map Maker forum

You can take a look at Google's official Map Maker discussion forums (`http://goo.gl/Wc9Zh`) and choose which forums and communities to join based on your interests. Here, you can post and share your experiences with fellow mappers across the world or within your region. The forum allows you to subscribe to discussions involving Map Maker and also have hearty exchanges and collaboration with fellow mappers around the world. Important updates and changes to Map Maker are communicated to the community through these forums as well.

Google Map Maker moderation guidelines

Take a look at the official guideline (`http://goo.gl/KbSdF`) for reviewing and moderating edits in Google Map Maker if you are in doubt or unsure of what and/or how to go about it.

Map Makerpedia

If your find yourself stuck or want to make reference on how to carry out some operation in Google Map Maker, this is the official repository and reference point for any of that (`http://goo.gl/yP8oG`).

Google Lat Long blog

If you want to stay informed with all the latest updates and changes to all of Google's Geo platforms including Google Map Maker, this blog (`http://google-latlong.blogspot.com/`) is the one you need to subscribe to and bookmark. Don't worry, it's not spam.

Map Maker Social

Follow Google Map Maker on Twitter at `https://twitter.com/googlemapmaker`, on Facebook at `https://www.facebook.com/GoogleMapMaker`, and on Google Plus at `https://plus.google.com/+GoogleMaps/posts` to stay updated with all the latest happenings in the world of maps and Map Maker. You can also watch all your favorite video tutorials about Map Maker on YouTube. Subscribe and follow the Map Maker Channel at `http://www.youtube.com/googlemapmaker`.

Downloading Google Map Maker data

Would you like to make a formal request to Google to download some of the data in Google Map Maker for non-commercial use? Put up your request (using this link: `https://services.google.com/fb/forms/mapmakerdatadownload/`) and explain why, who, and how you would like to use the data and Google will get back to and after ascertaining all the above, will avail to you the data for download in KML format. Read more on GIS data formats, here, at `http://en.wikipedia.org/wiki/GIS_file_formats`.

Watching live edits in Map Maker

Catch all the edits live in real time as they happen in Google Map Maker from here (`http://www.google.com/mapmaker/pulse`). This is my personal toy in Google Map Maker as it shows me the edits live as they happen and who is making them across the globe. The tool auto-pans across the regions as the edits keep coming through. Try it!

I wish you all the best in your mapping endeavors.

About Packt Publishing

Packt, pronounced 'packed', published its first book "*Mastering phpMyAdmin for Effective MySQL Management*" in April 2004 and subsequently continued to specialize in publishing highly focused books on specific technologies and solutions.

Our books and publications share the experiences of your fellow IT professionals in adapting and customizing today's systems, applications, and frameworks. Our solution based books give you the knowledge and power to customize the software and technologies you're using to get the job done. Packt books are more specific and less general than the IT books you have seen in the past. Our unique business model allows us to bring you more focused information, giving you more of what you need to know, and less of what you don't.

Packt is a modern, yet unique publishing company, which focuses on producing quality, cutting-edge books for communities of developers, administrators, and newbies alike. For more information, please visit our website: www.packtpub.com.

Writing for Packt

We welcome all inquiries from people who are interested in authoring. Book proposals should be sent to author@packtpub.com. If your book idea is still at an early stage and you would like to discuss it first before writing a formal book proposal, contact us; one of our commissioning editors will get in touch with you.

We're not just looking for published authors; if you have strong technical skills but no writing experience, our experienced editors can help you develop a writing career, or simply get some additional reward for your expertise.

OpenLayers 2.10 Beginner's Guide

ISBN: 978-1-84951-412-5   Paperback: 372 pages

Create, optimize, and deploy stunning cross-browser web maps with the OpenLayers JavaScript web-mapping library

1. Learn how to use OpenLayers through explanation and example

2. Create dynamic web map mashups using Google Maps and other third-party APIs

3. Customize your map's functionality and appearance

4. Deploy your maps and improve page loading times

OpenLayers Cookbook

ISBN: 978-1-84951-784-3   Paperback: 300 pages

60 recipes to create GIS web applications with the open source JavaScript Library

1. Understand the main concepts about maps, layers, controls, protocols, events etc

2. Learn about the important tile providers and WMS servers

3. Packed with code examples and screenshots for practical, easy learning

Please check **www.PacktPub.com** for information on our titles

Python Geospatial Development

ISBN: 978-1-84951-154-4   Paperback: 508 pages

Build a complete and sophisticated mapping application from scratch using Python tools for GIS development

1. Build applications for GIS development using Python

2. Analyze and visualize Geo-Spatial data

3. Comprehensive coverage of key GIS concepts

4. Recommended best practices for storing spatial data in a database

Programming ArcGIS 10.1 with Python Cookbook

ISBN: 978-1-84969-444-5   Paperback: 304 pages

Over 75 recipes to help you automate geoprocessing tasks, create solutions, and solve problems for ArcGIS with Python

1. Learn how to create geoprocessing scripts with ArcPy

2. Customize and modify ArcGIS with Python

3. Create time-saving tools and scripts for ArcGIS

Please check **www.PacktPub.com** for information on our titles

www.ingramcontent.com/pod-product-compliance
Lightning Source LLC
LaVergne TN
LVHW080106070326
832902LV00014B/2450